A Shorter Course in Everyday Conversation

5分間 英会話決まり文句 140

Hidehiko Konaka

NAN'UN-DO

Download Audio

音声ファイル
無料 DL
のご案内

このテキストの音声を無料で視聴（ストリーミング）・ダウンロードできます。自習用音声としてご活用ください。
以下のサイトにアクセスしてテキスト番号で検索してください。

https://nanun-do.com　テキスト番号［**512237**］

※ 無線 LAN（WiFi）に接続してのご利用を推奨いたします。

※ 音声ダウンロードは Zip ファイルでの提供になります。
お使いの機器によっては別途ソフトウェア（アプリケーション）の導入が必要となります。

Read by
Dominic Allen
Shizuka Anderson

※ A Shorter Course in Everyday Conversation 音声ダウンロードページは以下の QR コードからもご利用になれます。

A Shorter Course in Everyday Conversation

はじめに

国際化社会において、英語４技能のうちの「聞く」「話す」の２技能が持つ意味合いはますます大きくなっています。この２技能の基礎を築くためには、日常生活でよく使われる会話独特の「決まり文句」の習得が不可欠になります。本テキストはその日常生活でよく使われる「決まり文句」にスポットライトを当て、それらを習得することを目標に編集されています。

本テキストは20のレッスンで成り立ち、どのレッスンも同じ構成になっています。各セクションについて簡単に説明しておきます。

LET'S LEARN

日常よく使われる日常会話の決まり文句です。何度も音読して、会話表現を自分のものにしておきましょう。日本人が会話表現を聞き取るための豆知識もついています。

LET'S TRY

[A] 日本文をヒントに表現を完成させる「表現完成問題」です。
(LESSON 01-10 はカッコを、LESSON 11-20 は下線部を埋める問題です)

[B] 対話をヒントに適当な表現を選ぶ「表現選択問題」です。

[C] 対話をヒントにカッコを埋める「表現完成問題」です。

[D] 日本文を英語に直す「表現作文問題」です。

本テキストの編集にあたり、各種辞書類、会話教本など数多くの文献を参考にさせていただきました。本テキストはこれらの文献に負うところが多いことを記して謝辞といたします。

本テキストによって皆さんが英会話を学ぶ楽しさを感じ、さらに自主的に英会話を学んでみようという気持ちになってくれれば、これにすぎる喜びはありません。心から皆さんの健闘を祈っています。

最後になりましたが、本テキストの編集・出版にあたり、いろいろお世話になった南雲堂の加藤敦氏に深く感謝いたします。また、Michael P. Critchley 氏にすべての英文をていねいにチェックしていただき、適切なアドバイスもたくさんいただきました。ここに記して感謝の意を表します。

小中秀彦

目次

LESSON 01

YOU 中心の会話表現

● LET'S LEARN

001 After you. お先に行ってください。

［カフェテリアで］

A: Who's going to go first?（誰が先に並ぶの？）

B: *After you.*（お先にどうぞ）

002 See you. またね。

A: *See you*, Natalie.（ナタリー、またね）

B: OK. See you later.（オーケー。ではまた）

＊ ダジャレで、later と alligator（アメリカ・中国産のワニ）が韻を踏んで、See you later, alligator. ともいう。返事は、while と crocodile（アフリカ・オーストラリア産のワニ）が韻を踏んで、In a while, crocodile.（またね）という。

003 Thank you. ありがとう。

A: Had a good day?（楽しい１日だった？）

B: Very nice, *thank you*.（とてもよかったよ、どうもね）

＊ Thanks.、Thanks a lot.、Many thanks.、Thanks a million. などとも表現できる。

＊「A をありがとう」は Thank you for A. と表現する。

004 You can count on me. お任せください。

A: Will you help me move the sofa, Ted?（テッド、ソファーを動かすのを手伝ってくれない？）

B: Yeah. *You can count on me*.（いいよ。任せておいて）

005 You can say that again. あなたの言うとおりです。

A: Gee, it's cold today.（うわー、今日は寒いね）

B: *You can say that again*.（そのとおりだね）

＊ ＜ that again → tha*d*again ＞のように、「母音＋ [t] ＋母音」で [t] が「ダ」のような音に聞こえることがある。［例］Don't do that again.（二度とそんなことしちゃだめだよ）→ Don't do tha*d*again.

006 You're welcome. どういたしまして。

A: Thank you very much for the nice dinner.（すてきなディナーをどうもありがとう）

B: *You're welcome.*（どういたしまして）

＊ You're quite welcome.、Don't mention it.、No problem.、Sure.、It was nothing. などとも表現できる。

007 You've got a deal. これで話は決まった。

A: I'll take care of this if you buy me lunch tomorrow.（もし明日ランチをおごってくれたら、ここはぼくが払うよ。）

B: OK. *You've got a deal*.（いいよ。これで話は決まった）

■ LET'S TRY

[A] 日本語をヒントにカッコを埋め、表現を完成させなさい。

(1) またね。　(　　　　) (　　　　).

(2) お先にどうぞ。　(　　　　) (　　　　).

(3) お任せください。

(　　　　) (　　　　) (　　　　) (　　　　) (　　　　).

(4) あなたの言うとおりです。

(　　　　) (　　　　) (　　　　) (　　　　) (　　　　).

[B] 下線部に入る適当な表現を選びなさい。

(5) A: It must have been a boring job.

B: ________________

(A) Thank you.　(B) You can say that again.

(C) You've got a deal.

(6) A: Thank you for a great time this weekend.

B: ________________ I had a great time, too.

(A) You can say that again.　(B) You're welcome.

(C) You've got it.

[C] カッコを埋めて、表現を完成させなさい。

(7) A: You do the dishes, and I'll clean the room.

B: OK. (　　　　) (　　　　) (　　　　) (　　　　).

(8) A: Have a good time on your vacation. I'll be seeing you.

B: (　　　　) (　　　　) next week. Bye.

(9) A: I had a great time. (　　　　) (　　　　) (　　　　) the party last night.

B: Don't mention it. I'm glad you enjoyed it.

[D] 日本語を英語で表現しなさい。

(10) A: すてきな誕生日プレゼントをどうもありがとう。

____

B: どういたしまして。

____

命令文の会話表現 (1)

● LET'S LEARN

03

008 Be my guest. どうぞご遠慮なく／（勘定を）私持ちにさせてください。

A: I would just love to have some more cake, but there is only one piece left.（もう少しケーキをいただきたいけど、でも１つしか残ってないわ）

B: *Be my guest.*（どうぞご遠慮なく）

009 Excuse me. ちょっと失礼／ごめんなさい。

A: *Excuse me.* Could I get past?（ちょっと失礼。通していただけますか？）

B: Sure.（どうぞ）

＊ ＜ excuse → *'xcuse* ＞のように、あいまい母音は消えたように聞こえることがある。
［例］Excuse me.（ごめんなさい）→ *'xcuse* me.

＊ 相手のことばがよく聞き取れなかったとき、Excuse me? と上昇調で用いると、「何と言いましたか？；もう一度おっしゃってください」という意味になる。(I) Beg your pardon? とも表現できる。

010 Go ahead. どうぞ／やっていいよ。

A: Can I turn on the air conditioner?（エアコンつけてもいい？）

B: Sure. *Go ahead.*（いいよ。どうぞ）

011 Guess what! ねえねえ／何だと思う？

A: *Guess what!* Ed got married to Mary.（ねえねえ。エドがメアリーと結婚したのよ）

B: Really? I can't believe it.（本当？信じられないわ）

＊ 相手が驚くようなことを伝える前に、相手の注意を引くために使う。言われた方は、What? と言うか、黙って相手の顔を見てその先を言うのを待つ。

012 Help yourself. ご自由にどうぞ。

A: Can I have one of these doughnuts?（ドーナツ１つ食べてもいい？）

B: *Help yourself.*（どうぞご自由に）

＊「A［食べ物・飲み物］を自由にどうぞ」は Help yourself to A. と表現する。

013 Take your time. ごゆっくり。

A: I'll change and be ready in fifteen minutes.（15 分で着替えて用意するから）

B: *Take your time,* Matilda.（マチルダ、ごゆっくり）

014 Wait a minute. ちょっと待って。

A: *Wait a minute,* Jim. I need to buy some water.（ジム、ちょっと待って。お水、買わなきゃ）

B: Take your time. We've got lots of time.（どうぞごゆっくり。時間はたっぷりあるから）

＊ Just a minute. とも表現できる。

■ LET'S TRY

[A] 日本語をヒントにカッコを埋め、表現を完成させなさい。

(1) 何だと思う？　(　　　　) (　　　　)!

(2) やっていいよ。　(　　　　) (　　　　).

(3) ごゆっくり。　(　　　　) (　　　　) (　　　　).

(4) ちょっと待って。　(　　　　) (　　　　) (　　　　).

[B] 下線部に入る適当な表現を選びなさい。

(5) A: Can I say a few words before dinner?
B: Of course! ______________

(A) Be my guest.　(B) Wait a minute.
(C) Help yourself.

(6) A: Do you have any cola?
B: Yes, it's in the fridge. ______________

(A) Guess what!　(B) Help yourself.
(C) Take your time.

[C] カッコを埋めて、表現を完成させなさい。

(7) A: Could you pass me the mustard?
B: (　　　　) (　　　　)? I couldn't hear you.

(8) A: (　　　　) (　　　　)! I got the prize. A trip to Miami.
B: Really? I can't believe it.

(9) A: Please (　　　　) (　　　　) (　　　　) some more turkey.
B: Thank you.

[D] 日本語を英語で表現しなさい。

(10) A: ちょっと待って。着替えなきゃ。

____

B: どうぞごゆっくり。

____

LESSON
03 WHAT 中心の会話表現

● LET'S LEARN

015 What are you talking about? 何を言っているんだ？

A: Is she your girlfriend?（彼女、君のガールフレンド？）
B: *What are you talking about*? She's my sister.（何、言ってるんだ？妹だよ）

016 What can I do for you? 何かお役に立てますか？

A: *What can I do for you*?（ご用件は何ですか？［いらっしゃいませ］）
B: May I try this on?（これを試着してもいいですか？）

017 What do you think? どう思う？

A: *What do you think*, Ralph?（ラルフ、どう思う？）
B: I think you look wonderful in it.（それを着ているとすてきだよ）

＊ What do you say? とも表現できる。
＊「A はどう思いますか？」は What do you think of [about] A? と表現する。

018 What for? 何のために？

A: I'm going to San Francisco next week.（来週、サンフランシスコに行くんだ）
B: *What for*?（何しに？）

019 What makes you think so? どうしてそう思うの？

A: He's a real character.（彼って本当に味のある人だね）
B: *What makes you think so*?（どうしてそう思うの？）

＊ ＜ makes you → mak'*sju* ＞のように、「[s] + [j]」は「シュ」のような音に聞こえることがある。
［例］That suit makes you look much younger.（そのスーツを着ると君はずっと若く見えるよ）
→ That suit mak'*sju* look much younger.

020 What's the matter? どうしましたか？

A: *What's the matter*, Alice? You look a little pale.（アリス、どうしたの？少し顔色が悪いわよ）
B: I have a headache.（頭痛がするの）

＊ What's wrong? とも表現できる。
＊「A はどうしましたか？」は What's the matter with A? と表現する。

021 What's up? 何があったの？／元気にやっているかい？

A: *What's up*? There's an ambulance outside.（何があったの？外に救急車がいるけど）
B: Bill fell down and hit his head hard.（ビルが転んで、頭を強く打ったんだ）

＊ 何があったのか尋ねる場合と、相手の様子を尋ねる挨拶として用いる場合がある。

■ LET'S TRY

[A] 日本語をヒントにカッコを埋め、表現を完成させなさい。

(1) 何のために？　(　　　　) (　　　　)?

(2) 元気にやっているかい？　(　　　　) (　　　　)?

(3) どうしましたか？　(　　　　) (　　　　) (　　　　)?

(4) 何を言っているんだ？

(　　　　) (　　　　) (　　　　) (　　　　) (　　　　) (　　　　)?

[B] 下線部に入る適当な表現を選びなさい。

(5) A: We're considering moving out into the country. ____________________

B: Sounds good to me.

(A) What are you talking about?　(B) What can I do for you?

(C) What do you think?

(6) A: People shouldn't sit with their legs crossed in the subway.

B: ________________________ Is it uncomfortable?

(A) What for?　(B) What makes you think so?

(C) What's up?

[C] カッコを埋めて、表現を完成させなさい。

(7) A: May I ask a favor of you?

B: Yes. (　　　　) (　　　　) (　　　　) (　　　　) (　　　　)

(　　　　)?

(8) A: (　　　　) (　　　　)? There's a police car outside.

B: Thieves broke into Fred's house around midnight.

(9) A: (　　　　) (　　　　) (　　　　) (　　　　) (　　　　)

this weather?

B: Lovely weather for ducks.

[D] 日本語を英語で表現しなさい。

(10) A: ラルフ、どうしましたか？少し疲れているようですね。

____

B: 昨夜よく眠れなかったんです。

____

LESSON
04 主語 I の会話表現 (1)

● LET'S LEARN

022 I don't feel like it. ちょっとその気になれないよ。

A: Do you want to go to Las Vegas?（ラスベガスに行かない？）
B: No. I *don't feel like it.*（いいえ。今、その気になれないわ）

＊「ちょっと～する気じゃない」は I don't feel like *doing*. と表現する。
＊＜feel like → *fee'like*＞のように、同じ音が続くと、前の音が抜け落ちたように聞こえることがある。［例］I don't feel like eating.（今、食べたくないんだ）→ I don't *fee'like* eating.

023 I guess you're right. 君の言うとおりだ。

A: We should wash the car today.（今日、車洗わなきゃね）
B: *I guess you're right.* I'll do it this afternoon.（君の言うとおりだ。今日の午後ぼくがやるよ）

024 I have no idea. わかりません。

A: Where can I listen to some jazz live?（ジャズのライブを聴けるところってどこかしら？）
B: *I have no idea.*（見当もつかないよ）

＊ No idea. とも表現できる。

025 I hope so. そうだといいですね。

A: Will it be nice out tomorrow?（明日は晴れるかな？）
B: *I hope so.*（そうだといいですね）

＊ その内容が自分や相手にとって望ましいときに使う。
＊「そうでないといいですね」は I hope not. と表現する。

026 I know how you feel. お気持ちはわかります。

A: We're working longer hours for less pay.（長時間働いても稼ぎが少ないですよね）
B: *I know how you feel.* It's tough to work these days.（お気持ちはわかります。最近の労働はきついですよね）

027 I mean it. 本当だよ／本気だよ。

A: You're fired, Richard. *I mean it.*（リチャード、君はクビだ。本当だよ）
B: Are you kidding. Why?（うそでしょ。理由は？）

＊ 自分の言ったことや約束したことが「うそではない」「間違いなく本気だ」と伝えるときに使う。

028 I wish I could. できればいいんだけど。

A: Would you like to go shopping on Sunday?（日曜日に買い物に行かない？）
B: *I wish I could.* I have a test on Monday.（行けたらいいんだけど。月曜日にテストがあるの）

＊「行けない」という気持ちが背後にある。誘いをやんわり断るときにも使う。
＊「そうしたいのはやまやまですが…」は I wish I could, but... と表現する。... には節［文］がくる。

■ LET'S TRY

[A] 日本語をヒントにカッコを埋め、表現を完成させなさい。

(1) わかりません。 (   ) (   ) (   ) (   ).

(2) そうでないといいですね。 (   ) (   ) (   ).

(3) 君の言うとおりだ。 (   ) (   ) (   ) (   ).

(4) お気持ちはわかります。

(   ) (   ) (   ) (   ) (   ).

[B] 下線部に入る適当な表現を選びなさい。

(5) A: You want to marry me? You don't mean it, do you?

B: ________________________

(A) I don't feel like it.　　(B) I mean it.

(C) I wish I could.

(6) A: I've studied Spanish for four years, but I can't speak it well.

B: ________________________ It's hard to master a foreign language.

(A) I have no idea.　　(B) I hope so.

(C) I know how you feel.

[C] カッコを埋めて、表現を完成させなさい。

(7) A: Do you have any idea where Lucy is?

B: (   ) (   ) (   ) (   ).

(8) A: (   ) (   ) (   ) (   ) (   ).

B: Then how about something to drink?

(9) A: Are you going to be at my concert?

B: (   ) (   ) (   ) (   ), (   )

I have to be out of town.

[D] 日本語を英語で表現しなさい。

(10) A: ルーシー、土曜日にキャンプに行かない？

____

B: いいえ。今、その気になれないわ。

____

LESSON
05 名詞中心の会話表現 (1)

● LET'S LEARN

029 Cheers! 乾杯！

A: Let's drink to the happy couple.（幸せなカップルに乾杯しよう）
B: Right. *Cheers*!（そうだね。乾杯！）

＊「A に乾杯！」は Cheers to A! と表現する。

030 Congratulations! おめでとうございます！

A: I won the championship in the tennis tournament.（テニスの大会で優勝したんだ）
B: *Congratulations*! Well done.（おめでとう！よくやったね）

＊ 本来は努力に対して使う表現。新年・クリスマス・誕生日のあいさつには使わない。
＊「A おめでとう！」は Congratulations on A! と表現する。

031 My pleasure. どういたしまして／もちろん。

［病院で］
A: Oh, doctor, you've really helped Bob. Thank you so much!（ああ、先生、ボブを助けてくださいまして、本当にありがとうございます）
B: *My pleasure*.（どういたしまして）

032 No kidding! まさか！

A: I saw a UFO yesterday.（昨日、UFO を見たよ）
B: *No kidding*!（うそでしょ！）

＊ 耳を疑うような話を聞いたときに使う。You're kidding. とも表現できる。

033 No problem. いいですよ。

A: Sorry to bother you, but can I talk with you for a minute?（恐縮ですが、少しお話してよろしいですか？）
B: *No problem*. Have a seat.（かまいませんよ。お座りください）

034 No wonder. 道理でね。

A: Brad was born in Norway.（ブラッドはノルウェー生まれだよ）
B: *No wonder*. He can ski so well.（道理でね。だからスキーが上手いのか）

＊「道理で…」は No wonder... と表現する。

035 What a waste. もったいない。

A: Sue quit her job.（スーが仕事辞めたんだ）
B: *What a waste*.（なんてもったいない）

＊ ＜ what a → *whata* ＞のように、「[t] ＋母音」で音がつながったように聞こえることがある。
［例］What a beautiful day!（何ていい天気なんでしょう！）→ *Whata* beautiful day!

■ LET'S TRY

[A] 日本語をヒントにカッコを埋め、表現を完成させなさい。

(1) いいですよ。　　　　　(　　　　　) (　　　　　).

(2) もったいない。　　　　(　　　　　) (　　　　　) (　　　　　).

(3) みんなの健康に乾杯！　(　　　　　) (　　　　　) your health!

(4) ご昇進おめでとうございます！

(　　　　　　　) (　　　　　) your promotion!

[B] 下線部に入る適当な表現を選びなさい。

(5) A: ____________________ You have a healthy baby boy.

B: Thank you very much.

(A) Congratulations!　　　(B) My pleasure.

(C) No problem.

(6) A: I'm originally from Honolulu, but I live in Kamakura.

B: ____________________ I live there, too. What a coincidence!

(A) My pleasure.　　　(B) No kidding!

(C) What a waste.

[C] カッコを埋めて、表現を完成させなさい。

(7) A: Excuse me. May I have your autograph?

B: (　　　　　　) (　　　　　　).

(8) A: OK, everyone raise your glasses. Let's make a toast.

B: (　　　　　　)!

(9) A: (　　　　　　) (　　　　　　) (　　　　　　). It's bad for the environment.

B: Oh, sorry. I'll be careful next time.

[D] 日本語を英語で表現しなさい。

(10) A: スーはカナダ生まれだよ。

____

B: 道理でね。だから英語とフランス語が上手いのか。

____

LESSON 06

主語 IT の会話表現

● LET'S LEARN

07

036 Does it come with anything? それには何かついてきますか？

［レストランで］

A: *Does it come with anything*?（それには何かついてきますか？）

B: It comes with French fries.（フライドポテトがついてきます）

＊ レストランで注文の際、メニューの内容を確認する場合などに使う。

037 It figures. やっぱりね。

A: He had a car accident last week.（彼は先週、車で事故ったんだ）

B: *It figures*. He's a terrible driver.（やっぱりね。彼は運転が下手だからね）

＊ That figures. とも表現できる。

038 It sounds reasonable to me. それなら納得できます。

A: This is an 80-dollar-a-night hotel.（ここは１泊 80 ドルのホテルよ）

B: *It sounds reasonable to me*.（それなら納得できる値段だね）

039 It's OK. まあまあです／だいじょうぶ。

A: How was the movie, Wendy?（ウェンディ、映画はどうでした？）

B: *It was OK*, nothing special.（まあまあでした。特にどういうこともなく）

040 It's on me. 私のおごりです。

A: Want to have a drink, Robert?（ロバート、１杯やろうか？）

B: Yes. *It's on me*.（うん。ぼくがおごるよ）

＊ It's on the house.（店のおごりです）という表現もある。

041 It's so nice of you. ご親切にありがとう。

A: I'd like to give you a present.（君にプレゼントがあるんだ）

B: *It's so nice of you*.（ご親切にありがとう）

＊「～してくれてありがとう」は It's so nice of you to *do*. と表現する。

＊ ＜ it is → *it's* ＞のように、「主語＋ be 動詞」は短くなることがある。［例］It is cold today.（今日は寒い）→ *It's* cold today.

042 It's up to you. あなたが決めて。

A: Who should we invite to the party?（パーティーには誰をお招きしようかしら？）

B: *It's up to you*.（君にまかせるよ）

＊ You decide.（あなたが決めて）とも表現できる。

■ LET'S TRY

[A] 日本語をヒントにカッコを埋め、表現を完成させなさい。

(1) やっぱりね。　(　　　　)(　　　　).

(2) だいじょうぶ。　(　　　　)(　　　　).

(3) 私のおごりです。　(　　　　)(　　　　)(　　　　).

(4) それなら納得できる。

(　　　　)(　　　　)(　　　　)(　　　　)(　　　　).

[B] 下線部に入る適当な表現を選びなさい。

(5) A: Please use this dictionary as long as you like.

B: ____________________ I really appreciate your help.

(A) It sounds reasonable to me.　(B) It's so nice of you.

(C) It's up to you.

(6) A: We had a good lunch. How much is the check?

B: Oh, ____________________ today.

(A) it figures　(B) it's OK

(C) it's on me

[C] カッコを埋めて、表現を完成させなさい。

(7) A: I just want to apologize for being so cold to you last night.

B: (　　　　)(　　　　). We all have days like that.

(8) A: I'll have the seafood salad. (　　　　)(　　　　)(　　　　)

(　　　　)(　　　　)?

B: It comes with some bread.

(9) A: We can either stay at home and eat or go out to a restaurant.

B: You decide. (　　　　)(　　　　)(　　　　)(　　　　).

[D] 日本語を英語で表現しなさい。

(10) A: ステーキをお願いします。それには何かついてきますか？

____

B: パンとサラダがついてきます。

____

LESSON 07 I'M の会話表現

● LET'S LEARN

043 I'm a stranger here myself. 私もこのへんは不案内です。

A: Do you know a place where I can catch a taxi?（どこでタクシーをひろえますか？）
B: Sorry, *I'm a stranger here myself.*（ごめんなさい。私もこのへんは不案内なので）

044 I'm all ears. ちゃんと聞いていますよ。

A: Are you listening to me?（私の話、聞いているの？）
B: *I'm all ears.*（ちゃんと聞いていますよ）

＊ 直訳すると「全身が耳です」、つまりそのくらい集中して聞いているという意味。

045 I'm coming. 今行くよ。

A: Come downstairs, Allen. Dinner's ready.（アレン、降りてらっしゃい。夕食ができたわよ）
B: *I'm coming.*（今行くよ）

046 I'm glad to hear that. それを聞いてうれしい。

A: I got a job!（採用されたよ！）
B: Great! *I'm glad to hear that.*（すごい！それを聞いてうれしいわ）

047 I'm glad you like it. 気に入ってもらえてうれしい。

A: This is a beautiful tie! Thank you, Karen.（すてきなネクタイだね！カレン、ありがとう）
B: *I'm glad you like it.*（気に入ってもらえてうれしいわ）

048 I'm looking forward to seeing you. 会うのを楽しみにしています。

A: I'll be in Los Angeles in two weeks.（あと２週間でロサンゼルスにまいります）
B: *I'm looking forward to seeing you.*（お会いするのを楽しみにしています）

＊ 類似表現の、I'm looking forward to *working* with you.（いっしょに働ける［勉強できる］のを楽しみにしています）は、新しい同僚やクラスメイトが入ってきた場合などに、日本語の「どうぞよろしく」の意味で用いることがある。

049 I'm sorry. ごめんなさい。

A: Oh, *I'm sorry*. Did I step on your foot?（あ、ごめんなさい。足を踏みましたか？）
B: That's OK.（だいじょうぶですよ）

＊「〜してごめんなさい」は I'm sorry to *do*. と表現する。［例］I'm sorry *to have* kept you waiting so long.（長い間お待たせしてすみません）
＊「…のことはごめんなさい」は I'm sorry... と表現する。
＊ ＜ kept you → kep*tju* ＞のように、「[t] + [j]」は「チュ」のような音に聞こえることがある。［例］Sorry to have kept you waiting.（お待たせしちゃってごめんね）→ Sorry to have kep*tju* waiting.

■ LET'S TRY

[A] 日本語をヒントにカッコを埋め、表現を完成させなさい。

(1) ごめんなさい。 (　　　　) (　　　　).

(2) ちゃんと聞いてますよ。 (　　　　) (　　　　) (　　　　).

(3) それを聞いてうれしい。

(　　　　) (　　　　) (　　　　) (　　　　) (　　　　).

(4) 私もこのへんは不案内なので。

(　　　　) (　　　　) (　　　　) (　　　　) (　　　　).

[B] 下線部に入る適当な表現を選びなさい。

(5) A: Our dog finally died yesterday.

B: Oh, ____________________

(A) I'm coming. (B) I'm looking forward to seeing you.

(C) I'm so sorry.

(6) A: Thank you very much for your nice birthday present.

B: You're welcome. ____________________

(A) I'm a stranger here myself. (B) I'm all ears.

(C) I'm glad you like it.

[C] カッコを埋めて、表現を完成させなさい。

(7) A: Hurry up, will you?

B: OK. (　　　　) (　　　　).

(8) A: I got a job as a secretary.

B: Great! (　　　　) (　　　　) (　　　　) (　　　　)

(　　　　).

(9) A: Excuse me, but could you tell me the way to Lincoln Center?

B: I'm sorry. (　　　　) (　　　　) (　　　　) (　　　　)

(　　　　).

[D] 日本語を英語で表現しなさい。

(10) A: 今度の月曜日に東京にまいります。

____

B: お会いするのを楽しみにしています。

____

LESSON

08 否定命令文の会話表現

● LET'S LEARN

050 Don't be silly. バカなこと言わないで。

A: I can't stand his remarks. I'm going to quit right now.（やつの言いぐさには我慢できないよ。今すぐ辞めてやる）

B: *Don't be silly*. Just calm down.（バカなこと言わないで。まあ落ち着いて）

＊ ＜going to → *gonna*＞のように、going to は「ゴナ」のような音に聞こえることがある。［例］I'm going to be in a race tomorrow.（明日はレースに出るんだ）→ I'm *gonna* be in a race tomorrow.

051 Don't get me wrong. 誤解しないで。

A: You don't think I can handle the job, huh?（その仕事は私の手に負えないと思っているの？）

B: *Don't get me wrong*. I just said it's a difficult job.（誤解しないで。ただその仕事は難しいって言っただけよ）

＊ 自分が相手に誤解された、あるいは誤解されそうだ、と思ったときに使う。Don't take me wrong. とも表現できる。

052 Don't mention it. どういたしまして。

A: I really appreciate your kindness, Tess.（テス、親切にしていただき本当に感謝しています）

B: *Don't mention it*.（どういたしまして）

053 Don't rush me. そんなにせかさないで。

［レストランで］

A: The waiter wants to take your order. What do you want?（ウェイターが注文をとりたがっているよ。何にするの？）

B: *Don't rush me*. I can't make up my mind.（せかさないで。決められないのよ）

＊ rush を名詞として使い、There's no rush.（急ぐ必要はないよ）、What's the rush?（何でそんなにあわてているの？）のように使うこともできる。

054 Don't worry about it. 気にしないで。

A: I'm sorry I struck out, Chuck.（チャック、ごめん、三振しちゃった）

B: *Don't worry about it*.（気にしないで）

055 Never mind. 気にしないで。

A: What did you say?（えっ、何だって？）

B: *Never mind*. It wasn't important.（気にしないで。たいしたことじゃなかったの）

056 Never say die! 弱音をはかないで！

A: Oh, German is just impossible!（もう、ドイツ語はどうにも手に負えないよ）

B: *Never say die*!（弱音をはかないで！）

■ LET'S TRY

[A] 日本語をヒントにカッコを埋め、表現を完成させなさい。

(1) 弱音をはかないで！ ( ) ( ) ( )!

(2) どういたしまして。 ( ) ( ) ( ).

(3) バカなこと言わないで。 ( ) ( ) ( ).

(4) そんなにせかさないで。 ( ) ( ) ( ).

[B] 下線部に入る適当な表現を選びなさい。

(5) A: I just had another fight with Chuck.
B: ________________________ Everything will work out in the end.
(A) Don't be silly. (B) Don't worry about it.
(C) Never say die!

(6) A: Are you telling me we lost the data. How did it happen?
B: ________________________ The data isn't lost. We have a back-up.
(A) Don't get me wrong. (B) Don't mention it.
(C) Don't rush me.

[C] カッコを埋めて、表現を完成させなさい。

(7) A: I'm so slow. I'll never learn French.
B: ( ) ( ) ( ).

(8) A: We have to leave now.
B: ( ) ( ) ( ). There's a lot of time.

(9) A: I'm sorry. I broke one of your glasses.
B: ( ) ( ). It's nothing to worry about.

[D] 日本語を英語で表現しなさい。

(10) A: ソファーを動かすのを手伝ってくれてありがとう。

____

B: どういたしまして。

____

LESSON 09

主語 THAT の会話表現

● LET'S LEARN

057 That depends. 時と場合によります。

A: Can I see you again, Eddy?（エディ、また会えるかしら？）
B: *That depends.*（時と場合によるな）

＊後ろに、on circumstances が省略された形。単に、Depends.、または That all depends. とも表現できる。
＊「A 次第だ」は It depends on A. と表現する。

058 That looks very nice on you. あなたにとても似合いますよ。

A: I bought a new summer hat.（新しい夏用の帽子買ったんだ）
B: *That looks very nice on you.*（あなたによく似合うわ）

059 That makes sense. なるほど、道理に合ってますね。

［オフィスで］
A: She was late for work today.（彼女は今日、仕事に遅刻したんだ）
B: *That makes sense.* She watched TV all night.（道理で。一晩中テレビを見てたんだって）

060 That's for sure. それは確かです。

A: I never want to work with Sara again, *that's for sure.*（もうサラとは一緒に働きたくないよ。確かに）
B: Yeah, she can't do anything right.（そうだね。彼女は何もうまくできないからね）

061 That's too bad. それはいけませんね。

A: I have a slight fever.（少し熱があるんです）
B: Oh, *that's too bad.*（えー、それはいけませんね）

＊単に、Too bad. とも表現できる。
＊＜ have a → ha*v'a* ＞のように、「[v] ＋母音」で音がつながったように聞こえることがある。
［例］Have a good time.（楽しんでね）→ Ha*v'a* good time.

062 That's unbelievable! 信じられない！

A: Joe got fired for being five minutes late.（ジョーは5分遅刻しただけでクビになったんだ）
B: *That's unbelievable!*（信じられないわ！）

＊I can't believe it. とも表現できる。

063 That's why. それが理由です。

A: You look depressed.（落ち込んでいるみたいだね）
B: I failed the exam. *That's why.*（試験に落ちちゃったの。それが理由よ）

＊「そういうわけで…」は That's why... と表現する。

■ LET'S TRY

[A] 日本語をヒントにカッコを埋め、表現を完成させなさい。

(1) 時と場合によるな。 (　　　　) (　　　　).

(2) 信じられない！ (　　　　) (　　　　)!

(3) それはいけませんね。 (　　　　) (　　　　) (　　　　).

(4) なるほど、道理に合ってますね。 (　　　　) (　　　　) (　　　　).

[B] 下線部に入る適当な表現を選びなさい。

(5) A: Why do you always put your right shoe on first?
B: I always pick up the right one first. ________________

(A) That depends. (B) That's too bad.
(C) That's why.

(6) A: I wonder what I should wear today. I'll be making a presentation.
B: Choose something black. ________________

(A) That looks very nice on you. (B) That makes sense.
(C) That's unbelievable.

[C] カッコを埋めて、表現を完成させなさい。

(7) A: He's a very energetic person.
B: Yeah. (　　　　) (　　　　) (　　　　).

(8) A: Will you be able to come to the meeting this evening?
B: (　　　　) (　　　　).

(9) A: Eddy was playing baseball in the park.
B: (　　　　) (　　　　)! He broke his leg last week.

[D] 日本語を英語で表現しなさい。

(10) A: 明日は何を着たらいいかな。スピーチすることになっているんだ。

____

B: ブルーがいいと思うわ。あなたにとても似合うから。

____

LESSON 10

形容詞・副詞中心の会話表現

● LET'S LEARN

064 Certainly. もちろんいいですよ。

A: Could you do me a favor, Max?（マックス、お願いがあるのですが）
B: *Certainly*. What can I do for you?（もちろん。ぼくに何ができますか？）

＊ Sure (thing).、Sure enough. とも表現できる。
＊ ＜ could you → coul*dju* ＞のように、「[d] ＋ [j]」は「ジュ」のような音に聞こえることがある。
［例］ Could you put the light on?（明かりをつけていただけますか？）
→ Coul*dju* put the light on?

065 Good for you. よかったね。

A: I finally gave up smoking.（とうとうタバコをやめたんだ）
B: Oh, *good for you*.（へぇー、よかったわね）

066 Here you are. はい、どうぞ。

［レストランで］
A: Can I have the menu, please?（メニューを見せてください）
B: *Here you are*.（はい、どうぞ）

＊「人」に重点がある場合には、Here you are.、Here you go. が、「物」に重点がある場合には、Here it is. が用いられる。

067 Here's something for you. これあなたに。

A: *Here's something for you*. I hope you like it.（これ君に。気に入るといいんだけど）
B: Thank you so much.（どうもありがとう）

068 Nice meeting you. お会いできてうれしいです。

A: I must be going now. It was a wonderful party.（もう帰らないと。すばらしいパーティーでした）
B: *Nice meeting you*.（お会いできてうれしいです）

＊ Glad to have met you. とも表現できる。
＊ 出会ったときは、Nice to meet you.（はじめまして）、別れるときは、Nice meeting you. を用いる。

069 Same here. 同感だ。

A: I'm very hungry.（腹ペコだ）
B: *Same here*.（同じく）

070 Sounds good. いいね。

A: How about coming to our BBQ on Sunday, Cindy?（シンディ、日曜日のバーベキューに来ない？）
B: *Sounds good*.（いいわね）

＊ Sounds great.（すごくいいね）とも表現できる。

■ LET'S TRY

[A] 日本語をヒントにカッコを埋め、表現を完成させなさい。

(1) いいね。 (　　　　) (　　　　).

(2) よかったね。 (　　　　) (　　　　) (　　　　).

(3) はい、どうぞ。 (　　　　) (　　　　) (　　　　).

(4) お会いできてうれしいです。 (　　　　) (　　　　) (　　　　).

[B] 下線部に入る適当な表現を選びなさい。

(5) A: I just got a raise.
B: ____________________

(A) Nice meeting you. (B) Good for you.
(C) Here you are.

(6) A: Could you help me with the packages?
B: ____________________ Just pull your car up in front of the store.

(A) Certainly. (B) Here's something for you.
(C) Sounds good.

[C] カッコを埋めて、表現を完成させなさい。

(7) A: Could you give me a ride home?
B: (　　　　). No problem.

(8) A: (　　　　) (　　　　) (　　　　) (　　　　).
B: Oh, how sweet of you. May I open it now?

(9) A: I think math class is too difficult.
B: (　　　　) (　　　　). His explanations are hard to follow.

[D] 日本語を英語で表現しなさい。

(10) A: マックス、放課後テニスをしない？

____

B: いいね。

____

LESSON
11 LET'S・PLEASE 中心の会話表現

● LET'S LEARN

071 Let's call it a day. 今日はこれでおしまいにしよう。

A: *Let's call it a day*. I'm tired.（今日はこれで終わりにしよう。疲れたよ）
B: Me too. Let's get out of here.（ぼくもだ。ここを出よう）

072 Let's get started. さあ、始めましょう。

A: Everybody is here and the drinks are ready.（みんなそろって、飲み物も用意できているね）
B: OK. *Let's get started*.（オーケー。始めましょう）

073 Let's split the bill. 割り勘にしましょ。

A: How much is it, Michael? *Let's split the bill*.（マイケル、いくらなの？割り勘にしましょ）
B: OK. That's 12 dollars each.（1人 12 ドルずつだよ）

074 Let's take five. 少し休憩しよう。

A: It's so hot today, isn't it?（今日は本当に暑いですね）
B: Yes, indeed. I'm kind of thirsty. *Let's take five*.（ええ、まったく。ちょっとのどが渇いてきたわ。ちょっと休憩しましょう）

＊ 休憩時間は必ずしも５分でなくてもいい。
＊ ＜kind of → *kindof*＞のように、「[d] ＋母音」で音がつながったように聞こえることがある。
［例］It's kind of you to come and see me.（会いに来てくださってありがとうございます）
→ It's *kindof* you to come and see me.

075 Please don't. おやめください。

［レストランで］
A: Are you finished?（食事はおすみですか？）
B: *Please don't*.（持っていかないで）

＊「～しないようにお願いします」は Please don't *do*. と表現する。

076 Please don't bother. どうぞおかまいなく。

A: Let me get a glass of iced coffee for you.（アイスコーヒーを入れてきましょう）
B: *Please don't bother*, Laura.（ローラ、どうぞおかまいなく）

077 Please make yourself at home. どうぞ楽になさってください。

A: Come in. *Please make yourself at home*.（中に入って。どうぞ楽になさってください）
B: Thank you. I'd like to.（ありがとう。そうしたいわ）

＊ Please make yourself comfortable. とも表現できる。

■ LET'S TRY

[A] 日本語をヒントに下線部を埋め、表現を完成させなさい。

(1) さあ、始めましょう。 ________________________________.

(2) 割り勘にしましょう。 ________________________________.

(3) どうぞおかまいなく。 ________________________________.

(4) どうぞ楽になさってください。 ________________________________.

[B] 下線部に入る適当な表現を選びなさい。

(5) A: Come in, Michael. ____________________ I've got a few things to do.
B: Nice place you've got here.

(A) Let's call it a day. (B) Please don't bother.
(C) Please make yourself at home.

(6) A: ____________________
B: No. It was my idea to have dinner tonight. Let me take care of it.

(A) Let's get started. (B) Let's split the bill.
(C) Let's take five.

[C] カッコを埋めて、表現を完成させなさい。

(7) A: May I take photos here?
B: ( ) ( ).

(8) A: Well, that's the end of the reports. Nothing else to do.
B: ( ) ( ) ( ) ( ) ( ).

(9) A: I want to have some coffee.
B: Me too. ( ) ( ) ( ).

[D] 日本語を英語で表現しなさい。

(10) A: 熱い緑茶が飲みたいわ。

____

B: ぼくも。少し休憩しよう。

____

LESSON
12 命令文の会話表現 (2)

● LET'S LEARN

078 Believe me. 私の言うことを信じて。

A: What? The hall has accommodation for 900 people? It can't be true.（何ですって？そのホールは 900 人収容できるの？ありえない話だわ）

B: *Believe me*. I saw the ad today.（ぼくの言うことを信じて。今日その広告を見たんだ）

079 Enjoy your stay. 滞在中、楽しんでください。

A: I'll be in San Diego for another week.（サンディエゴにあと１週間います）

B: Oh, I need to get off here. *Enjoy your stay*.（おっと、ここで降りなきゃ。滞在中、楽しんでください）

＊ ＜need to→nee*d*to＞のように、似た音が続けば前の音が抜け落ちたように聞こえることがある。［例］We need to take a break.（私たちは休憩をする必要がある）→ We nee*d*to take a break.

080 Give it a try. やってみなよ。

A: Is that a new video game?（それ新しいテレビゲーム？）

B: Yeah. Come on. *Give it a try*.（うん。ほら。やってみなよ）

081 Let me see. ええと。

A: Where did you see Lisa?（どこでリサを見かけたんですか？）

B: *Let me see*. In the library.（ええと。図書館です）

＊ Let's see. とも表現できる。

082 Say hello to him. 彼によろしく言って。

A: I've got to go. I'm meeting Henry at five.（もう行かなくちゃ。５時にヘンリーと会うの）

B: *Say hello to him*.（彼によろしく言って）

083 Say when. いいっていうとき言って。

A: I've never had *sake* before. Let me try some. Just a little.（日本酒は飲んだことないわ。試しに飲んでみるわ。ちょっとだけね）

B: OK. *Say when*.（いいわ。いいっていうとき言ってね）

＊ 飲み物を注ぎながら分量について用いる。答えは、OK.、That's enough. など、ふざけた感じに When. と答えることもある。

084 Tell me. 教えて。

A: *Tell me*, Frank. Is he married?（フランク、ちょっと教えて。彼、結婚している？）

B: Yes, he is.（うん、しているよ）

＊「A について教えて」は Tell me about A. と表現する。

■ LET'S TRY

[A] 日本語をヒントに下線部を埋め、表現を完成させなさい。

(1) ええと。 ______________________________.

(2) 私の言うことを信じて。 ______________________________.

(3) 滞在中、楽しんでね。 ______________________________.

(4) 彼によろしく言って。 ______________________________.

[B] 下線部に入る適当な表現を選びなさい。

(5) A: Is this your new bike?
B: Yeah. ____________________

(A) Believe me. (B) Give it a try.
(C) Tell me.

(6) A: Please show me where we are on this map.
B: ____________________ We are here on this street.

(A) Enjoy your stay. (B) Let me see.
(C) Say when.

[C] カッコを埋めて、表現を完成させなさい。

(7) A: (　　　　) (　　　　).
B: That's enough, thanks.

(8) A: (　　　　) (　　　　) (　　　　) your company.
B: Well, it's a small publishing house.

(9) A: Do you think I should enter the race next week?
B: Absolutely! (　　　　) (　　　　) (　　　　) (　　　　).

[D] 日本語を英語で表現しなさい。

(10) A: もう行かなくちゃ。6時にフランクと会うの。

____

B: 彼によろしく言って。

____

LESSON 13

HOW・WHY 中心の会話表現

● LET'S LEARN

085　How about you?　あなたはどう？

A: How have you been, Sally?（サリー、元気でやってた？）
B: Not bad. *How about you*?（まあまあね。あなたは？）

＊「A はどうですか？」は How about A? と表現する。
＊「～するのはどうですか？」は How about *doing*? と表現する。
＊＜ about you → about*ju* ＞のように、「[t] + [j]」は「チュ」のような音に聞こえることがある。
　[例] How about you?（君はどう？）→ How about*ju*?

086　How are you doing?　どう、元気？

A: *How are you doing*, Kay?（ケイ、どう、元気？）
B: Not bad, and you?（元気よ、あなたは？）

＊ How are you?（ごきげんいかがですか？）よりもややくだけた表現。

087　How come?　どうして？

A: I don't want to go to the summer camp.（サマーキャンプには行きたくないな）
B: *How come*, Tom? You're looking forward to it.（トム、どうして？楽しみにしてたじゃない）

＊「どうして…なの？」は How come...? と表現する。

088　How do you feel?　気分はどうですか？

A: *How do you feel* today?（今日はご気分はいかがですか？）
B: Much better, thank you.（おかげさまでずっとよくなりました）

＊ How are you feeling? とも表現できる。
＊「A のことをどう思う？」は How do you feel about A? と表現する。

089　How do you know?　どうしてわかるの？

A: The train is about to pull into the station.（電車がすぐに駅に入ってくるよ）
B: *How do you know*?（どうしてわかるの？）

090　How would you like your eggs?　卵の調理法はどういたしましょう？

[ホテルのレストランでの朝食で]
A: *How would you like your eggs*?（卵はどのように調理いたしましょうか？）
B: Sunny-side up, please.（目玉焼きにしてください）

＊ ステーキの焼き加減を聞くときには、How would you like your steak? を使う。

091　Why not?　もちろん／なぜいけないの？

A: Would you lend me your pen, please?（あなたのペンを貸してもらえる？）
B: *Why not*?（もちろんどうぞ）

■ LET'S TRY

[A] 日本語をヒントに下線部を埋め、表現を完成させなさい。

(1) どうして？ ______________________________?

(2) なぜいけないの？ ______________________________?

(3) どう、元気？ ______________________________?

(4) どうしてわかるの？ ______________________________?

[B] 下線部に入る適当な表現を選びなさい。

(5) A: How would you like your eggs?
B: ____________________

(A) Medium rare, please. (B) Scrambled, please.
(C) With rice, please.

(6) A: I have to apologize for the coffee. It probably isn't very good.
B: ____________________

(A) How are you doing? (B) How do you know?
(C) How do you feel?

[C] カッコを埋めて、表現を完成させなさい。

(7) A: You shouldn't read that magazine.
B: (   ) (   )?

(8) A: (   ) (   ) (   ) on a picnic?
B: That's a good idea.

(9) A: (   ) (   ) (   ) (   )?
B: I had a good sleep and feel much better.

[D] 日本語を英語で表現しなさい。

(10) A: サリー、今日のご気分はいかがですか？

____

B: 昨夜、十分睡眠をとったので、ずっと気分がいいです。

____

LESSON 14

主語 I の会話表現 (2)

● LET'S LEARN

15

092 I can't believe it. そんなこと信じられない。

A: My dad is fifty eight.（うちのパパは 58 才だよ）
B: *I can't believe it.*（信じられない）

＊ ＜ believe it → belie*v'it* ＞のように、「[v] ＋母音」で音がつながったように聞こえることがある。
［例］I can't believe it.（そんなこと信じられない）→ I can't belie*v'it*.

093 I can't help it. しょうがない。

A: Shhh!（シーッ！）
B: I'm sorry for laughing. *I can't help it.*（笑ってしまってすみません。こらえきれなくて）

＊ It can't be helped. とも表現できる。

094 I can't wait. 待ちきれないな。

A: Tomorrow is Christmas.（明日はクリスマスだね）
B: *I can't wait.*（待ちきれないな）

＊ I can hardly wait. とも表現できる。

095 I feel out of place. 場違いな感じだ。

A: Wow! You're so dressed up, Irene.（わー！アイリーン、ドレスアップしたのね）
B: I thought it was a formal party. *I feel out of place.*（形式ばったパーティーだと思ったの。場違いな感じね）

096 I really appreciate it. 本当にありがとう。

A: Thank you so much for everything. *I really appreciate it.*（いろいろありがとう。本当に感謝しているわ）
B: That's what friends are for.（友だちはそのためにいるんだから）

097 I used to. 昔はね。

A: Do you have a pet, Scott?（スコット、ペット飼ってる？）
B: *I used to.*（昔はね）

098 I wish you luck. うまくいくように。

A: I'll do my best in the contest.（コンテストではベストを尽くすよ）
B: *I wish you luck*, Vincent.（ビンセント、うまくいくよう祈っているわ）

■ LET'S TRY

[A] 日本語をヒントに下線部を埋め、表現を完成させなさい。

(1) 昔はね。 ______________________________.

(2) うまくいくように。 ______________________________.

(3) 場違いな感じね。 ______________________________.

(4) 本当にありがとう。 ______________________________.

[B] 下線部に入る適当な表現を選びなさい。

(5) A: My cat likes you more than me.
B: ______________

(A) I can't help it. (B) I can't wait.
(C) I feel out of place.

(6) A: Thank you for everything, Vincent. ______________
B: It's my pleasure. Happy to do it.

(A) I can't believe it. (B) I really appreciate it.
(C) I wish you luck.

[C] カッコを埋めて、表現を完成させなさい。

(7) A: He doesn't like me.
B: ( ) ( ) ( ) ( ).

(8) A: This lake is nearly 200 feet deep.
B: ( ) ( ) ( ) ( ).

(9) A: We'll be staying at a hot spring overlooking the ocean.
B: Sounds good. ( ) ( ) ( ).

[D] 日本語を英語で表現しなさい。

(10) A: スピーチコンテストではベストを尽くすわ。

____

B: アイリーン、うまくいくよう祈っているよ。

____

LESSON
15 名詞中心の会話表現 (2)

● LET'S LEARN

099 Good luck. がんばって。

A: *Good luck*, Dave.（デーブ、がんばって）
B: Thanks.（ありがとう）

∗「A をがんばって」は Good luck with A. と表現する。

100 Long time, no see. しばらくぶりだね。

A: Look who's here!（誰かと思えば！）
B: Wow! *Long time, no see*.（わー！しばらくぶりだね。）

∗ 正式には、I haven't seen you for a long time. という。

101 My goodness! おや、まあ！

A: *My goodness*! You sure bought a lot of bags.（あら、まあ！たくさんのバッグを買ったのね）
B: I got them at a sale.（バーゲンで買ったの）

∗ 関心や軽い驚きを表す一般的な表現。

102 No sweat. 楽勝だよ。

A: Would you help me complete these papers?（書類の記入を手伝ってもらえますか？）
B: *No sweat*.（お安いご用です）

∗ ＜ would you → would*dju* ＞のように、「[d] + [j]」は「ジュ」のような音に聞こえることがある。
[例] Would you mind waiting a minute, please?（少々お待ちいただけますか？）→ Would*dju* mind waiting a minute, please?

103 No way! 絶対にダメ／まさか！

A: You don't want any more sweet potatoes, do you?（もうサツマイモ、欲しくはないよね）
B: *No way*!（いらないわ！）

104 The same to you. そちらにも。

A: Merry Christmas, Nancy.（ナンシー、メリークリスマス！）
B: *The same to you*.（そちらにも、メリークリスマス！）

∗ You too. とも表現できる。

105 Way to go! よくやった！

A: Guess what! I've got a new job.（何だと思う。新しい仕事に就いたんだ）
B: Wow! *Way to go*!（わー。よくやったわね！）

∗ 立派な仕事を続けるように人を励ます表現。That's the way to go! とも表現する。
∗ (That's the) Way to go! は「そこだ、行け」「やれやれ」という意味でも使われる。

■ LET'S TRY

[A] 日本語をヒントに下線部を埋め、表現を完成させなさい。

(1) 楽勝だよ。 ____.

(2) 絶対にダメ！ ____!

(3) がんばって。 ____.

(4) よくやった！ ____!

[B] 下線部に入る適当な表現を選びなさい。

(5) A: Hey! ____________________
B: Yeah. How have you been?
(A) Long time, no see. (B) My goodness!
(C) No sweat.

(6) A: I just won two tickets to the Super Bowl. Want to go?
B: ____________________ What a good friend I have!
(A) Good luck. (B) The same to you.
(C) Way to go!

[C] カッコを埋めて、表現を完成させなさい。

(7) A: Have a nice day, Dave.
B: (   ) (   ) (   ) (   ).

(8) A: (   ) (   ) (   ) your date.
B: Thanks, Ellie. I'm really nervous.

(9) A: (   ) (   )! It's a diamond, isn't it?
B: Yes, it's your birthstone.

[D] 日本語を英語で表現しなさい。

(10) A: 誰かと思えば。しばらくぶりだね。

____

B: そうだね。元気だった？

____

LESSON 16

主語 YOU の会話表現

● LET'S LEARN

106　Are you all right?　だいじょうぶ？

A: You look pale, Hank. *Are you all right*?（ハンク、顔色が悪いわよ。だいじょうぶ？）
B: I felt dizzy, but now I'm fine, thank you.（ちょっとめまいがしましたが、もうだいじょうぶです、ありがとう）

＊ Are you OK? とも表現できる。
＊ That's all right.（いいんですよ；どういたしまして）という表現もある。

107　Are you sure?　確かですか？

A: He got promoted to manager.（彼、部長に昇進したんだ）
B: *Are you sure*?（間違いない？）

＊「…は確かですか？」は Are you sure…? と表現する。

108　Can you make it?　来られる？

A: We're planning a party at my apartment this coming Friday. *Can you make it*?（今度の金曜日にぼくのアパートでパーティーをやるつもりなんだ。君は来られる？）
B: I sure can.（もちろんよ）

109　Do you have anything in mind?　何か思っているものはありますか？

［お店で］
A: I'm looking for a present for my girlfriend.（ガールフレンドにプレゼントをさがしています）
B: *Do you have anything in mind*?（何か思っているものはありますか？）

110　Do you need some help?　何かお困りですか？

［お店で］
A: *Do you need some help*?（何かお困りですか？）
B: No, thank you. I'm just looking.（だいじょうぶです。見ているだけですから）

＊ ＜looking → *lookin'*＞のように、「ルッキン」のような音に聞こえることがある。［例］I'm just looking.（見ているだけです）→ I'm just *lookin'*.

111　Do you really think so?　本当にそう思いますか？

A: That dress looks good on you, Betty.（ベティー、あのドレス、君にとても似合っているよ）
B: *Do you really think so*?（本当にそう思う？）

112　You know what?　ねえ、ちょっと。

A: *You know what*? Your hair needs cutting.（ねえ、ちょっと。君、髪切らなきゃね）
B: So what?（だからどうだって言うんだ）

＊ You know something? とも表現できる。

■ LET'S TRY

[A] 日本語をヒントに下線部を埋め、表現を完成させなさい。

(1) 確かですか？ ____________________________?

(2) 来られる？ ____________________________?

(3) 本当にそう思いますか？ ____________________________?

(4) 何か思っているものはありますか？ ____________________________?

[B] 下線部に入る適当な表現を選びなさい。

(5) A: ____________________

B: Yes. I just got some scratches.

(A) Are you all right?　　(B) Are you sure?

(C) Do you really think so?

(6) A: ____________________

B: Why, thank you. These bags are actually quite heavy.

(A) Can you make it?　　(B) Do you have anything in mind?

(C) Do you need some help?

[C] カッコを埋めて、表現を完成させなさい。

(7) A: Ken will go back to Japan next week.

B: (　　　　) (　　　　) (　　　　)?

(8) A: (　　　　) (　　　　) (　　　　)? I'm falling in love with you.

B: I don't know what to say.

(9) A: (　　　　) (　　　　) (　　　　) (　　　　)? You sound terrible.

Did you catch a cold?

B: Yeah. I think I did. I have a sore throat.

[D] 日本語を英語で表現しなさい。

(10) A: ベティー、顔色が悪いよ。だいじょうぶ？

____

B: 胃が痛いんです。

____

LESSON 17

助動詞中心の会話表現

● LET'S LEARN

113 Could you spare me a few minutes? 少しお時間をいただけますか？

A: *Could you spare me a few minutes*?（ちょっとお時間をいただけますか？）
B: Yes, of course.（いいですよ、どうぞ）

＊ Could you spare a few minutes for me? とも表現できる。

114 May I ask you a question? 質問してもいいですか？

A: *May I ask you a question*, Paul?（ポール、質問していいですか？）
B: Yes, please. Ask me any question.（どうぞ。どんな質問でもいいですよ）

115 May I leave him a message? 彼に伝言をお願いしていいですか？

A: *May I leave him a message*?（彼に伝言をお願いしていいですか？）
B: Certainly.（いいですとも）

＊ May I leave a message for him? とも表現できる。

116 Will you check it? 調べていただけますか？

［お店で］
A: I found the earphones didn't work. *Will you check them*?（イヤホンが作動しないんです。調べていただけますか？）
B: Certainly. Wait a second, please.（かしこまりました。少々お待ちください）

117 Will you pick me up? 車で迎えに来てくれますか？

A: *Will you pick me up* at the station at eight o'clock?（８時に駅まで車で迎えに来てくれる？）
B: Yes. Of course.（うん。もちろん）

118 Would you do me a favor? ちょっとお願いがあるんですが。

A: Excuse me, but *would you do me a favor*?（ちょっとお願いがあるのですが）
B: Sure, Jane. What can I do for you?（ジェーン、いいよ。あなたのために私は何ができますか？）

＊「お願い、～してもらえる？」は Would you do me a favor and *do*? と表現する。

119 Would you mind opening the window? 窓を開けてくださいますか？

A: *Would you mind opening the window*?（窓を開けてくださいますか？）
B: No, not at all.（いいですよ）

＊ Would you mind *do*ing?（あなたは～することを気にしますか？）の表現で依頼されたら、No, not at all.、Of course not.、Certainly not. などの否定文で答えれば、引き受けたことになる。
＊ ＜mind → *min'*＞のように、単語の最後の破裂音は消えたように聞こえることがある。［例］Mind your step.（足元注意！）→ *Min'* your step.

■ LET'S TRY

[A] 日本語をヒントに下線部を埋め、表現を完成させなさい。

(1) 調べてもらえますか？ ______________________________?

(2) 彼に伝言をお願いしていいですか？ ______________________________?

(3) 窓を閉めてくださいますか？ ______________________________?

(4) ちょっとお時間をいただけますか？ ______________________________?

[B] 下線部に入る適当な表現を選びなさい。

(5) A: May I ask you a question, Jane?
B: ____________________

(A) Go ahead.　　(B) No, thank you.
(C) Of course not.

(6) A: ____________________
B: Sorry, I do mind. I have a sore throat.

(A) May I leave him a message?　　(B) Will you check it?
(C) Would you mind opening the window?

[C] カッコを埋めて、表現を完成させなさい。

(7) A: (　　　) (　　　) (　　　) (　　　) a few minutes?
B: Sure. What is it?

(8) A: (　　　) (　　　) (　　　) (　　　) (　　　) at my house at six?
B: Certainly.

(9) A: (　　　) (　　　) (　　　) (　　　) (　　　) (　　　) (　　　) mail this letter?
B: Yes, of course.

[D] 日本語を英語で表現しなさい。

(10) A: 電卓が作動しないんです。調べていただけますか？

____

B: かしこまりました。少々お待ちください。

____

LESSON 18

副詞中心の会話表現

● LET'S LEARN

120　Just a little.　ちょっとだけ。

A: Is there any jam left?（ジャムは残っていますか？）
B: Yes, *just a little*.（ええ、少しだけ）

121　Leaving so soon?　もうお帰りですか？

A: *Leaving so soon*, Tom?（トム、もう帰るの？）
B: Yes, thanks for inviting me. I really have to go.（うん、招いてくれてありがとう。本当に行かなきゃいけないんだ）

122　Me too.　私も。

A: I hope it doesn't rain.（雨が降らないといいけど）
B: *Me too*.（そうですね）

＊ Me too. は肯定文を受ける。否定文を受ける場合には、Me neither. を使う。

123　Not too bad.　まあまあです。

A: Hello, Kate. How are you?（やあ、ケイト。元気かい？）
B: *Not too bad*, thanks.（まあまあよ、ありがとう）

124　Not yet.　まだです。

[レストランで]
A: Are you finished?（お食事おすみですか？）
B: No, *not yet*.（いいえ、まだです）

＊ ＜ not yet → no*tje* ＞のように、「[t] + [j]」は「チェ」のような音に聞こえることがある。
［例］Not yet.（まだです）→ No*tje*.

125　So far so good.　これまでは順調です。

A: How's the project going?（プロジェクトの進み具合は？）
B: *So far so good*.（今のところ順調です）

126　Sure.　もちろん／どういたしまして。

A: Can I leave my bag here?（カバンをここに置いていってもいいですか？）
B: *Sure*.（もちろん）

＊ Sure thing.、Sure enough. とも表現できる。

■ LET'S TRY

[A] 日本語をヒントに下線部を埋め、表現を完成させなさい。

(1) まだです。 ________________________________.

(2) どういたしまして。 ________________________________.

(3) ちょっとだけ。 ________________________________.

(4) これまでは順調です。 ________________________________.

[B] 下線部に入る適当な表現を選びなさい。

(5) A: I don't like that song very much.
B: ____________

(A) Me neither. (B) Me too. (C) Not yet.

(6) A: Good evening, Kate. How are you?
B: ____________ I felt a little dizzy this morning, but I'm all right now.

(A) Just a little. (B) Not too bad. (C) Sure.

[C] カッコを埋めて、表現を完成させなさい。

(7) A: Can I have another cup of coffee?
B: (   ).

(8) A: I'm sorry I have another appointment.
B: (   ) (   ) (   )? I wish you could stay longer.

(9) A: How are you getting on with the new project?
B: (   ) (   ) (   ) (   ).

[D] 日本語を英語で表現しなさい。

(10) A: トム、おはようございます。お元気ですか？

____

B: まあまあです。昨夜、微熱があったんですが、もうだいじょうぶです。

____

LESSON
19 I'LL の会話表現

● LET'S LEARN

127 I'll be glad to. よろこんで。

A: Would you explain this English to me?（この英語を私に説明していただけますか？）
B: *I'll be glad to.*（よろこんで）

＊ ＜ glad to → gla*d*to ＞のように、似た音が続けば前の音が抜け落ちたように聞こえることがある。
［例］I'll be glad to.（よろこんで）→ I'll be gla*d*to.

128 I'll be staying until Saturday. 今週の土曜日までおります。

A: How long are you staying in New York?（ニューヨークにはどれぐらいご滞在ですか？）
B: *I'll be staying until Saturday.*（今週の土曜日までおります）

129 I'll miss you. 君がいなくなると寂しくなる。

A: *I'll miss you* very much, Brad.（ブラッド、寂しくなるわね）
B: I'll miss you, too.（ぼくも寂しいよ）

＊ しばらく会えなくなる人との別れのあいさつ。

130 I'll pass. やめておきます。

A: How about coffee, Maggie?（マギー、コーヒーはいかが？）
B: *I'll pass.*（結構です）

131 I'll show you around. ご案内しましょう。

A: This is my first visit to Kobe.（神戸は今回が初めてなんです）
B: OK. *I'll show you around* all the famous sights of Kobe.（オーケー。では私が神戸の名所を全部ご案内しましょう）

132 I'll tell you what. こうしたらどうかな／ちょっと聞いて。

A: *I'll tell you what.* Let's buy some sandwiches and eat outside.（こうしたらどうかな。サンドイッチを買って外で食べようよ）
B: Good idea.（いいわね）

＊ 提案をする際のくだけた前置き。

133 I'll think about it. 考えておきます。

A: Do you want to take a helicopter tour?（ヘリコプターツアーに行きたくないですか？）
B: *I'll think about it.*（考えておきます）

＊「～しようと思っている」は現在進行形を用いて、I'm thinking about *do*ing. と表現する。

■ LET'S TRY

[A] 日本語をヒントに下線部を埋め、表現を完成させなさい。

(1) 考えておきます。 ________________________________.

(2) こうしたらどうかな。 ________________________________.

(3) 君がいなくなると寂しくなる。 ________________________________.

(4) 今週の土曜日までおります。 ________________________________.

[B] 下線部に入る適当な表現を選びなさい。

(5) A: We have about two hours to kill.
B: ________________ There's an art museum near here. Let's go there.
(A) I'll be glad to. (B) I'll tell you what.
(C) I'll think about it.

(6) A: Ann brought a chocolate cake. Would you like some, Brad?
B: Looks good, but ________________ I'm still on a diet.
(A) I'll be glad to. (B) I'll miss you.
(C) I'll pass.

[C] カッコを埋めて、表現を完成させなさい。

(7) A: I'm going back to Boston next month.
B: (　　　　　) (　　　　　) (　　　　　).

(8) A: Could you put these bags in my car for me?
B: Sure. (　　　　　) (　　　　　) (　　　　　) (　　　　　).

(9) A: (　　　　　) (　　　　　) (　　　　　) retiring and going to Palm Beach this year.
B: Are you serious?

[D] 日本語を英語で表現しなさい。

(10) A: 京都は今回が初めてなんです。

____

B: オーケー。では私たちが京都の有名な神社仏閣を全部ご案内しましょう。

____

LESSON 20

命令文の会話表現 (3)

● LET'S LEARN

134 Check it out. 試してみて。

A: Have you been to that new café near the station?（駅の近くにあるあの新しいカフェ、もう行ったの？）

B: Yeah. The coffee's good. *Check it out.*（うん。コーヒーがおいしいんだ。試しに行ってみて）

135 Give me a break. かんべんしてよ。

A: Let's eat Chinese food tonight.（今夜は中華料理を食べようよ）

B: Oh, *give me a break*. We've already had Chinese food three times this week!（えー。かんべんしてよ。今週は３回も中華料理を食べたじゃない）

136 Have fun. 楽しんでね。

A: I'm leaving for the picnic now.（さあ、ピクニックに出かけるよ）

B: *Have fun.*（楽しんでね）

137 Oh, come on. そんなこと言わないで。

A: You're so beautiful tonight, Cathy.（キャシー、今夜君は美しいね）

B: *Oh, come on.* Flattery won't get you anywhere.（やめて。お世辞言ってもむだよ）

138 Spit it out. はっきり言って。

A: Well, you know.... It's kind of hard to say....（あのー、ええと…ちょっと言いにくいんだけど…）

B: Come on, George. *Spit it out.*（ジョージ、何なの。はっきり言ってよ）

139 Take care of yourself. お体お大事に。

A: Don't worry. I'll get better soon.（心配しないでね。すぐよくなるから）

B: Well, *take care of yourself.*（それじゃあ、お体お大事に）

＊ Take care.（じゃあ、また）は親しい人との別れ際に使う。

＊ ＜ take care → *ta'care* ＞のように、同じ音が続くと、前の音が抜け落ちたように聞こえることがある。［例］I'll take care of the check.（勘定はぼくが払うよ）→ I'll *ta'care* of the check.

140 Take it easy. 気楽にね／じゃあね。

A: Don't worry about such trivial things. *Take it easy.*（そんなささいなことをくよくよしないで。気楽にね）

B: OK. Thanks.（うん。ありがとう）

■ LET'S TRY

[A] 日本語をヒントに下線部を埋め、表現を完成させなさい。

(1) 楽しんでね。 ______________________________.

(2) はっきり言って。 ______________________________.

(3) かんべんしてよ。 ______________________________.

(4) お体お大事に。 ______________________________.

[B] 下線部に入る適当な表現を選びなさい。

(5) A: It's hot and I'm getting tired.
B: ______________ Don't give up. We're almost there.

(A) Check it out. (B) Oh, come on.
(C) Spit it out.

(6) A: Did you know you ran a red light at that intersection?
B: ______________, officer. I swear the light was green.

(A) Give me a break (B) Take care of yourself
(C) Take it easy

[C] カッコを埋めて、表現を完成させなさい。

(7) A: See you next week, George.
B: (   ) (   ) (   ).

(8) A: We're going to go see a movie tonight.
B: (   ) (   ), Cathy.

(9) A: I feel much better than yesterday.
B: (   ) (   ) (   ) (   ) because it's getting cold.

[D] 日本語を英語で表現しなさい。

(10) A: 駅前のあの新しいイタリアンレストラン、もう行ったの？

____

B: うん。食べ物がおいしいんだ。試しに行ってみて。

____

INDEX

A Shorter Course in Everyday Conversation [B-971]
5分間 英会話決まり文句140

1 刷 2024年2月14日

著 者 小中 秀彦 Hidehiko Konaka

発行者 南雲一範 Kazunori Nagumo
発行所 株式会社 南雲堂
〒162-0801 東京都新宿区山吹町361
NAN'UN-DO Co., Ltd.
361 Yamabuki-cho, Shinjuku-ku, Tokyo 162-0801, Japan
振替口座：00160-0-46863
TEL: 03-3268-2311（営業部：学校関係）
03-3268-2384（営業部：書店関係）
03-3268-2387（編集部）
FAX: 03-3269-2486

編集者 加藤 敦
表 紙 Nスタジオ
組 版 Office haru
検 印 省 略
コード ISBN978-4-523-17971-9 C0082

Printed in Japan

E-mail nanundo@post.email.ne.jp
URL https://www.nanun-do.co.jp/